# Grateful Bob

## The Beginning...

By: Bob Briggs
Illustrated By: Bobby Briggs

Copyright © 2015 Bob Briggs

All rights reserved.

**ISBN-13: 978-1512311174**
**ISBN-10: 1512311170**

DEDICATION

I want to dedicate this series to my wife Julann and my 3 amazing children, Bobby, Ryan and Rylie. Without them, I would never be the person I am today. I owe every bit of my wonderful life to each of them. My "Grateful Bob" series is more of a reflection of what I have learned in my own life as I grow with these amazing individuals. I love you all so much!

The Beginning:

Learning what it means to be grateful.

Family and Friends

Believe it or not, when Bobby was just a baby, he was already learning how to be grateful.

When his Mommy would pick him up to play, or feed him, it made him feel warm and safe. It made him feel good, and feeling good is a way of being grateful.

Bobby is grateful for his Mommy.

Sometimes when Bobby woke up, Daddy was already gone.
He never knew where Daddy was for so long.

But everyday, Daddy would come home
and give him the biggest smile and hugs.

This made Bobby feel very special.
Feeling special is another way of being grateful.

So sometimes, Bobby would have his friend Tommy come over. They would play with the toys all day. Sometimes he would get upset when his friend would not give him the toy he wanted, so he would be sad.

But then, Tommy gave the toy back!

Was it because Bobby was sad?
I think it was because he just likes him.

"Next time, I will let him play with that
toy all day, because he is my good friend."
Bobby thought to himself

" Having a good friend makes us all Happy too! "

What friends are you grateful for?

I am grateful for my friend _____

Bobby just turned 2. He has already learned that some things make him happy, and some things make him sad.

Why should Bobby be grateful when he is sad?

 Sometimes when you are sad, something good happens next!

When Bobby was sitting in his high chair,
he knocked his milk right on to the floor.

"Oh no! said Bobby. "I spilled my milk!"

This made Bobby very sad. He was just about to get upset

when Mommy took out a new cup

and more milk out of the refrigerator.

Luckily, his Mommy had more milk for him.

Bobby drank his milk and was

so happy that his belly was full.

He watched his Mommy clean up the mess with a smile.

She was such a nice Mommy!

What foods are you grateful for?_____

When Bobby's Daddy saw him playing in the mud with his new shirt, he smiled and got down in the mud with him. This made Bobby giggle, and he smudged mud onto Daddy's nose. After, they went to the washing machine and washed their clothes. When Mommy came home, Bobby's new shirt looked new again.

"It's a good thing Daddy knows how to wash shirts!" said Bobby

"I bet Daddy is grateful for our washing machine. I know I am!"

What do your parents do for you sometimes?

11

Today Bobby found out he is going to be a big brother. Bobby was excited and sad at the same time.

He wanted a little brother but, "What if it was a girl?" Bobby wondered.

When Mommy came home from the hospital,
Bobby was nervous.
When they walked through the door, Daddy said
"Meet your little brother Ryan."

Bobby was so excited.
Mommy put the new baby on Bobby's lap.
He could not belive he had a new baby brother
He knew they were going to be best friends.
Do you have a brother, sister or cousin that you love?

Who is it? _____

Bobby really loved his brother. One day, Ryan got really sick. Mommy put something in his mouth to see how hot he was. Bobby was nervous because Ryan had to go to the doctor. Bobby did not like the doctor.

Bobby was so grateful that the doctor helped his little brother.

**What is the name of your doctor?**

_____

Bobby almost never got sick. He really likes to eat fruits and vegetables.
Bobby learned that fruits and veggies grow out of the ground.
He wanted to see it, so mommy and daddy took him
and his brother to a farm.

Bobby could see apple trees, plum trees,
grape vines and watermelons.
On the other side he saw corn, squash,
broccoli, lettuce and tomatoes.

He could not believe all the work the farmer did to get all that yummy food in his belly.
He was so happy that farmers work so hard.
He is so grateful for all the farmers.

What is your favorite fruit or vegetable?

_____

Bobby has 2 sets of Grandparents.

His Mommy's parents live right down the street,

but his Daddy's parents live
all the way in North Carolina.

He loves his Grandparents but
only see's his Mommy's parents.

He get's to talk to his Daddy's
parents once a week on the phone.

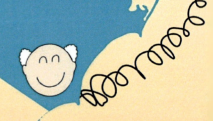

Papa is Bobby's grandfather down south.
Papa and Bobby laugh all the time.
Bobby is grateful he at least get's to speak with him on the phone.
"I am so lucky to have such loving grandparents." said Bobby.
Bobby is very grateful that his other grandparents live so close.

Where do your grandparents live?

_____

Now that Bobby is almost 3 years old, he has learned that having so many fun and loving people in his life makes him feel really good.
And when he feels really good inside, he knows it is because he is

# GRATEFUL

for all of them.

# Grateful Notes

21

What did Bobby learn so far?  Let's look back at some of the things that Bobby is grateful for.

1. Having a Mommy and Daddy that love you, make you smile and give the biggest hugs and kisses.
2. Even though Daddy goes to work for long hours sometimes, he always comes home to make me laugh and feel loved.
3. Having a best friend Tommy is awesome and he shares with me too. I am grateful for Tommy and for being able to share with a friend.
4. Bobby now knows that just because something bad happens, it does not mean something good can't happen right after.  You don't have to cry over spilled milk.
5. Bobby is grateful for being able to play in the mud with Daddy and that Daddy knows how to get his shirt clean for Mommy.
6. Bobby was so happy when he found out about his baby brother Ryan.
7. Sometimes Doctors can seem scary, but Bobby was grateful that the Doctor was able to help Ryan feel better.
8. Bobby did not know where all the fruits and veggies came from until he visited a farm with Mommy and Daddy.  Now he is grateful for farmers and all of their hard work.
9. Bobby really loves all of his grandparents.  He has a special relationship with Papa on the phone.  He is not sad that Papa  lives so far away. He is grateful that he get's to talk with him every week on the phone.

**Sometimes the bad things force you to recognize the good things in your life.**

List 10 things that you are grateful for in your life.

1_____  2_____
3_____  4_____
5_____  6_____
7_____  8_____
9_____  10_____

List 10 things that you forget to be grateful for sometimes.

1_____  2_____
3_____  4_____
5_____  6_____
7_____  8_____
9_____  10_____

### Daily Affirmations:

Today I am grateful for all of the bad things that I can learn from and all of the good things that help me.

I am grateful for the people in my life that love me for who I am.

I am grateful for the air that I breathe each day.

*"Be grateful for small things, big things, and everything in between. Count your blessings, not your problems."*

Mandy Hale

*Grateful Bob wants you to feel grateful everyday about something. Even if you are having a bad day, find one little thing to be grateful for and smile.*

Book 2 Coming Soon

Grateful Bob
Goes to School
Visit: www.gratefulbob.com

Made in the USA
San Bernardino, CA
30 September 2015